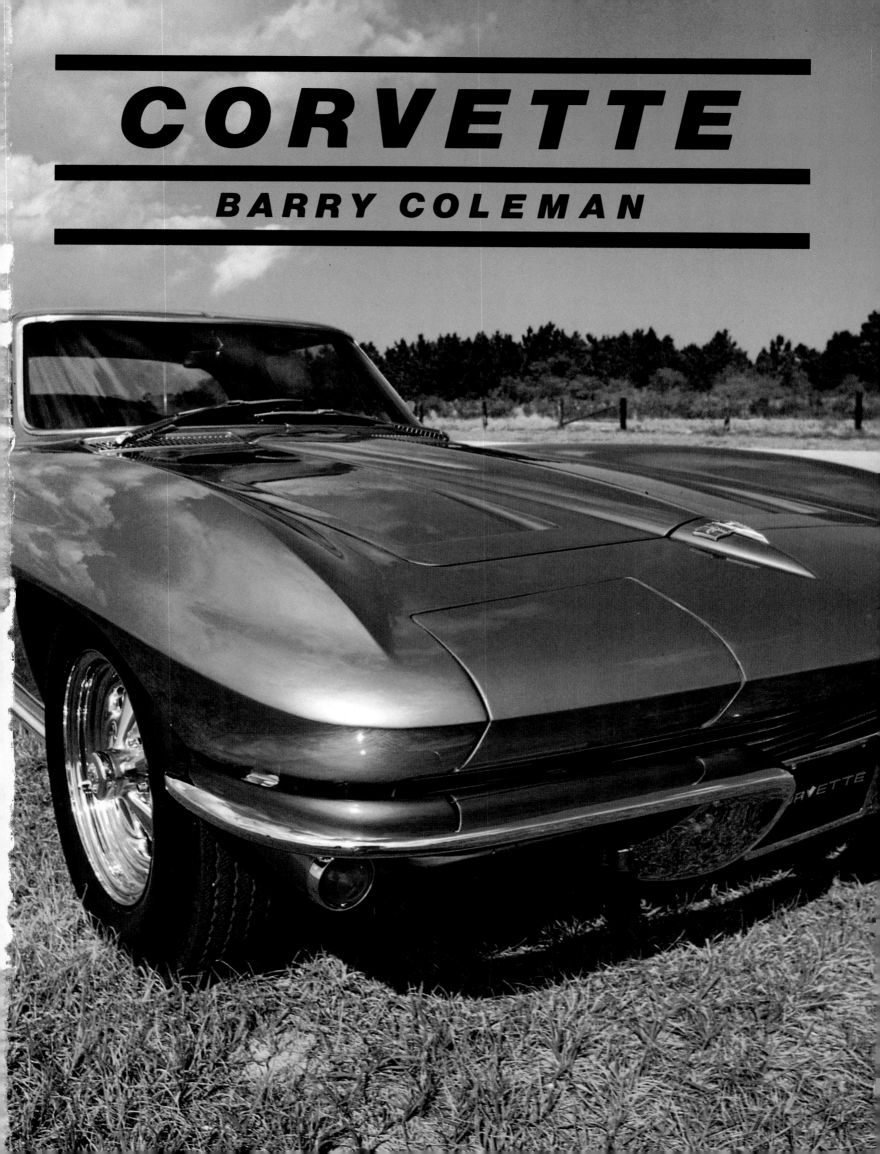

CORVETTE

BARRY COLEMAN

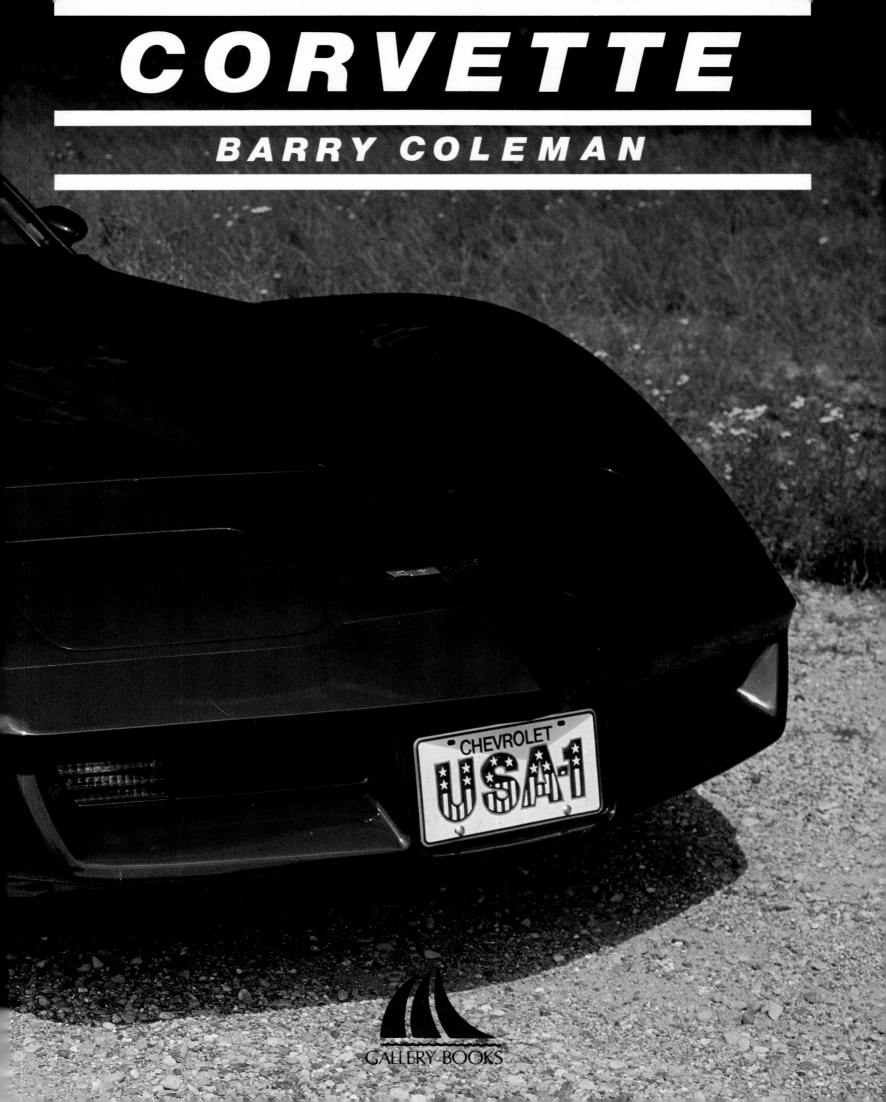

CORVETTE

BARRY COLEMAN

CHEVROLET

USA-1

GALLERY BOOKS

Copyright © 1983 by
Winchmore Publishing Services Limited

First Published in United States of America 1983
Second Impression 1983

Published by Gallery Press
An imprint of W.H. Smith
Publishers Inc.
112 Madison Avenue
New York, New York 10016

Manufactured in Spain
Printed by Graficromo s.a.

Designed by Laurence Bradbury
Produced by
Winchmore Publishing Services Limited
40 Triton Square
London NW1

1 2 3 4 5 6 7 8 9 10

Library of Congress Cataloging in
Publication Data

ISBN 0-8317-1791-2

CONTENTS

The story of the Corvette is. no doubt. familiar to the legions of its admirers. who are the real key to the amazing success of the car itself. In many ways the car tells its own story. Every minute styling change, every click up or down in the bhp figures, every twist in the development of its engineering, however slight or however radical. is visible in the profiles over the years.

In fact every one of those changes, for better or worse. reflects a decision taken. a battle won or lost. an ambition fulfilled or a hope smashed, a good idea wasted, or a bad one immortalized. Moreover, it is not the simple story of how a gigantic corporation, apparently in the face of every board-room and checkbook principle it ever held dear, took to an interesting. indeed exciting idea with all the gleeful en-thusiasm of an adolescent.

The production of the Corvette by General Motors was a remarkable piece of corporate behavior, and perhaps one that should make us look again at the assumptions we normally make about massive corporations. When General Motors

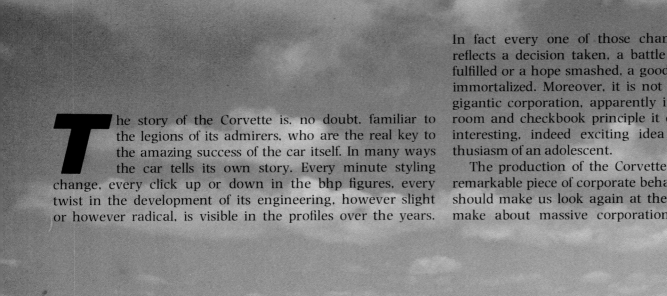

made the unexpected decision to proceed with the Corvette, it moved like lightning; and when General Motors became proud, in the ordinary, downhome way, of its sporting off-spring, it saw to it that the Corvette quickly reached the leading edge of world car design, and stayed there, year after year.

If a corporation can be said to have a personality or character of its own, it must of course originate with the ambitions and the talents of the people of which it is composed. It is not always easy, or even possible, to be sure which development, or lack of it, was inspired by an individual, or by the inscrutable workings of the great corporation itself.

Stunning on the street, fast and successful on the track, the 1962 Corvette was the mature sports car America had always wanted.

CHAPTER 1

THE LONG ROAD TO PRODUCTION

The Corvette is generally awarded the distinction of being America's only true sports car. That is, in itself, a claim that is open to a lot of questions but if we accept the definition, and ignore for the moment the low-volume, high-performance cars that Briggs Cunningham and others made, let us agree that the Corvette stands alone.

If that is the case then it is nothing short of dumbfounding. The United States is certainly more tied up with the automobile than any other nation, and it is a commonplace that the whole of the modern economy is based on the car. More to the point Americans like cars; they are interested in cars, they admire cars, and they celebrate the presence of cars in everyday life in an enormous variety of ways. From cruisers and rods to cowboy pickups and status-seeking luxury sedans, the precise nature and specification of cars appear to be important to a large number of Americans in a fairly fundamental way.

Then how is it that the Corvette is America's only real sports car? Why did the United States take so long to produce it?

The romantic interpretation of the Corvette's history is, broadly speaking, that in about 1952 a bunch of true-grit automobile engineers and stylists who just happened to be working at Chevrolet saw their chance and slipped one in on the huge General Motors Corporation and by the time it realized what it had done the true vehicle of the American Dream, the Chevrolet Corvette, was already in production.

There is another view, which is perhaps more interesting, and sheds more light not just on the Corvette's birth, but on its survival. In 1952 two powerful traditions in the American approach to the automobile finally merged at Chevrolet and produced something that the American car enthusiast really wanted — and had wanted for a long time.

When Louis Chevrolet and Billy Durant, who had set up the Chevrolet Company in 1911, parted in 1914 it was not merely the result of a personality clash. Louis Chevrolet the racer and engineering genius could not accept the irresistible logic of car production and marketing in the USA, a logic which, significantly, differed from that which operated in the older industrialized nations in Europe.

Neither Louis nor his brother, Arthur Chevrolet, had the breadth of vision to foresee how they could make excellent cars in the context of mass production. For them it must have seemed a pretty straightforward choice between quality and volume, between imagination and flair and heavy-handed production techniques. If the Chevrolet brothers could have foreseen the production techniques that developed after the Second World War and that exist today, they might have taken a slightly different view. They made their choice in the light of what was available, and they set off in pursuit of their own variety of excellence — an excellence that, interestingly, was immediately translated into speed.

They made the Fronty racing cars well enough for Louis' younger brother, Gaston, to win the 500-mile race at Indianapolis twice in 1920 and 1921. With Cornelius van Ranst, Louis Chevrolet went on to produce a number of remarkable engines, and a series of potent conversions for the Model T Ford. Very soon after they set up on their own and began thinking about the obvious: how to get a Frontenac onto the road. They talked to Stutz about it and the idea of making a sports car began to take off.

The deal with Stutz fell through, Louis realized that he was, by his own choice, divorced from the production technology he needed. In fact all over the United States brilliant auto engineers wanted to make sports cars but, like Louis, they were on their own. The production equipment they needed to make affordable cars and make ends meet was all tied up with massive finance. Massive finance wanted massive output and ever-declining unit costs, which meant the family car. This

Previous page: America's sports car in the making. The first Corvette was a showpiece sensation, but far from certain to become a racer.

Below: The Blue Flame Six had 235 cubic inches of displacement, compression ratio of 8:1, and an output of 150bhp at 4200rpm.

Bottom: Ready for the fray: General Motors took the Corvette from the drawing board to the street in a matter of months.

was what Billy Durant and the DuPonts, who had acquired Durant's General Motors Company which incorporated the Chevrolet Company, were interested in. They did not care about sports cars. The auto business was not about making sports cars, but about production. Any excellence was to be achieved in production techniques.

Making commercial metal of individual sports-car dreams just did not work in America. Low-volume production may have been possible in England, and say, Italy, because they are smaller, tighter-knit nations with more firmly-established tastes and preferences, of the kind that can be identified and commercially catered for. What characterized the growth of the American car market is that while it was inventing its auto industry, America was at the same time inventing itself. Such is the nature of a young nation: flexible, but moving too fast to explore every interesting diversion. The spur to speed, to breathtaking speed in this particular case, was competition.

However the history of the US automotive industry has not always been one of success. In 1921 Chevrolet was a commercial disaster and losing $5,000,000 a year. Hapless Chevrolet was nearing collapse when a bright young executive by the name of Alfred P Sloan stepped in to save it. DuPont, the new owner of General Motors and therefore of Chevrolet, agreed to give the miscreant another chance, but only if it produced a car which rivaled the Model T.

By 1923 Chevrolet was ready with the 490 Superior. Executive, rather than engineering decisions produced this, the first Chevy to give Henry Ford a hard time, since the changes to the original 490 were minimal, and centered on noise reduction. There were, thereafter, bad boardroom decisions and good ones, but Chevrolet was pointing in the right direction. In 1927 Chevrolet was outselling Ford by virtue of a quirk, but by 1931 it was firmly in the lead. In the years that followed, Ford was only able to take back the market lead on three occasions.

In those first triumphant years, a new stylist was working on the Chevys, a man who knew how to make a relatively modest car look like its more glamorous and expensive relatives, the Cadillacs and the Buicks. The name of this smart young man, who knew how to make something look good, who knew what would make it sell, was Harley Earl.

While Earl was learning how to influence and anticipate taste by the judicious application of styling, and General Motors was learning to trust the judgment that really did sell cars — the sports-car tradition of the hot but independent engineers was still alive and, in its way, well.

There were the sports cars of antiquity, the pre-First World War Locomobiles, Loziers, Stutzes, and T-head Mercers, which, in terms both of intention and efficiency were a distinctly mixed lot, and between the wars there were the quasi-sports Auburns, Cords, and Duesenbergs and the truly sporting Stutzes and DuPonts. What they represented, mainly, was engineering for engineering's sake allied to sport for sport's sake. It was not until the late 1940s that a faint but general clamor for an American sports car began to be heard through the specialist press. This mounting plea, little more at first than a muttering in the ranks, was important. Partially because it pointed to a shift in automotive taste, but more importantly, because it was soon loud enough to be heard in Detroit.

In the early 1950s the engineers and the engineer-racers were making good and interesting sports cars and near-sports

cars. A sports car, after all, is something you can drive to the supermarket or race at Le Mans. Sports cars usually incorporate two seats in their definition, so Frank Kurtis' lovely 1949 model was a sports car, but when he sold out and it took on two more seats under its new owner it became just a terribly fast convertible, the Muntz Jet.

Briggs Cunningham was at heart a racer, and he made big, powerful sports cars that were successful on the track at home and abroad but nothing more than fire-breathing rarities on the road. Nonetheless, Cunningham was at the heart of a great American tradition, and his exploits were invaluable in the development of the American sports car. In 1950, Cunningham raced two Cadillacs at Le Mans, and one of those who was only too interested in helping him was one of Cadillac's senior engineers, Edward N Cole. In 1952 Cunningham was at Watkins Glen racing his sports cars when GM's chief stylist, Harley J Earl, showed up to launch his latest two-seater dream car, the extravagant LeSabre. 'Oh come on, Harley,' Briggs had said with a provocative grin, 'when are you guys going to build a real sports car?'

There were Crosley Hotshots, Nash-Healeys, and then there was Kaiser-Frazer's decidedly hot Henry J. Any number of interesting specials were built on the chassis of the Henry J, but none was more interesting than the Kaiser-Darrin, which sported, of all things, a plastic body. Glass reinforced plastic, that is, GRP — fiberglass.

Fiberglass had been around for a while, and both the Second World War and the Korean war had intensified interest in its potential, not least in the automotive field. It was, however, a boat-builder, Bill Tritt, of Montecito, California, who finally proved its potential. Tritt and his associates fulfilled, in association with the US Rubber Company, a project which had begun as a commission to knock the square edges off the Jeep of a certain Mrs Brooks and ended with the presentation of a striking plastic-bodied sports car, the Alembic 1, to none other than General Motors.

Life magazine had been very taken with the plastic body of the Alembic, and so, in turn, were the smart engineers at Chevrolet. They had read *Life's* account, and had been to see Tritt even before the Alembic appeared in GM Styling's viewing auditorium, where it was thoughtfully examined by Harley J Earl.

Suddenly sports cars were everywhere. First Briggs Cunningham and his taunts, and now this. It was just as well, perhaps, that Earl had already started a tentative sports-car project, because suddenly it became an important sports-car project. Earl, the man who knew how to make an inexpensive car look good and sell well, had for some time been casting around for a way to make an imaginative, sporty little car in relatively small numbers at a reasonable price and had realized it had to be done with glass reinforced plastic.

Earl had a good team working on his sportster idea, but it would probably have ended up as little more than a slightly awkward amalgam of his disparate likings for the Jaguar XK120 and Willey's Jeepster, had it not been for the intervention of a clever young Cal Tech graduate called Bob McLean. Fortunately, McLean had never designed a whole car before and, for perfectly good reasons, he assumed, wrongly, that it was standard practice to start at the back. He placed the seats as close as he could get them to the rear axle, and, that done, he shuffled the engine as tight as it

would go up to the firewall.

When the Head of Styling came by, he seemed pleased. The wheelbase was 102 inches, and the upshot was long and low, very much to Earl's taste. Indeed, as he saw it, to the US public's taste. It was, as it turned out, the same wheelbase as the Jaguar and the much-admired MGs, and it would lend itself to the geometry of a very competitive sports car. More to the point was that the proposed chassis would enable Styling to give the Corvette a real character of its own. Which meant that Harley Earl would be able, perhaps, to sell it to his senior colleagues.

Chevrolet's new chief engineer Ed Cole was a sports car enthusiast and he was delighted by the whole idea. Cole promised his active support, and Earl went ahead, presiding first over the styling of a clay, and then of a fully-painted plaster mock-up. In April 1952, just a couple of months after he had first seen the Alembic 1, Harley Earl was ready to suggest to General Motors that the Chevrolet division should mass produce a plastic-bodied sports car. Earl pulled back the curtains in his viewing auditorium to reveal the Corvette, complete with a mannequin racer. His audience was very impressed; and his audience was the president of General Motors, Harlow 'Red' Curtice, and the general manager of

Left: Quick engine and snappy trim — the vital ingredients of the new sports car.

Below: Under the influence of Harley Earl, the Polo White '53 looked long, low, and expensive.

Chevrolet, Thomas Keating. The decision was made at once to make the Corvette the Chevrolet show car of 1953, so that a car that could be driven, if not exactly raced, had to be made in a little under seven months.

Tom Keating's reign at Chevrolet had, so far, been characterized by caution and conservatism. The Chevy range had become dull and everyone knew it. Curtice and Keating, of course, trusted Earl's skills and judgment, and saw the Corvette as the perfect car to put some excitement into the Chevrolet range. The Corvette was to be Chevrolet's contribution to the 1953 GM Motorama, a regular automotive extravaganza in cars, words, and music that opened in New York and then hopped across the country, through such cities as Kansas City and Chicago, to wind up on the West Coast a couple of months later. The Motoramas were an ingenious forum for GM both to dazzle the car-buying public and to garner valuable information about that public's reaction to what it saw.

Almost miraculously, the Corvette was ready in time for the 1953 Motorama. The effort, by Styling, by Engineering, and by individuals like Ed Cole and Research and Development chief Maurice Olley was truly remarkable. It underlined the fact that the weight of the corporation was behind the Corvette. Chevrolet and General Motors were beginning to believe not just in the Corvette, but in the American sports car.

It was a time of change and innovation. The fact that men like Tom Keating appeared to be changing the habits of a life-

time in supporting this dashing, imaginative venture revealed the fact that the product managers were waking up to the youth market (and even if the Corvette were not to prove a big seller, its appearance would at least signal to the youngsters of America that Chevrolet was their kind of car maker), and that the production engineers had foreseen the possibilities of cost-efficient, low-volume, almost specialist production offered by the new material, GRP. As it turned out, there were other production problems, and other materials would probably have been as useful, but it all showed that Chevrolet, and indeed US car manufacturers in general, were in a position where they were not only able, but actually obliged to think again about what the United States wanted.

The first Corvette was in fact a very tentative compromise, and bears little resemblance to today's Corvettes. It was low, shapely, and sophisticated, bearing features such as Earl's wrap-round windshield, push-button door catches, and a number of nicely-judged styling touches. The front end, with its bar grille and its caged-in headlamps, was suavely aggressive, and its interior trim was generous, almost luxurious. It looked a little heavy, by European standards, but it had clean lines and it had only two seats — bucket seats. It was, no doubt about it, an American sports car.

Of course, a Motorama show car was no plaster shell. The Corvette's body was indeed of GRP (something that caused considerable excitement in itself, and scored any number of points for GM as being adventurous and nicely abreast of developments) and its chassis was of a competely new and very interesting specification. It had box-section side members stiffened by an X-member; it was always intended to go fast. Front suspension was modified Chevrolet, but the rear end was new, featuring a conventional Hotchkiss drive, and leaf springs located outside the chassis side-members, again, for added stability at high speed.

What the Corvette needed was a sports-car engine, but Chevrolet did not have a suitable one. What they did have was the standard Chevy six, so Ed Cole set about making it fast. It was a strong engine, and it would stand quite a dramatic improvement in its efficiency. Cole imported a high-lifting, long duration camshaft and added solid valve lifters and dual-rate valve springs; the compression ratio was raised from 7.5:1 to 8:1, and the cooling system was uprated. Three Carter YH carburetors handled induction, breathing from the side in order to fit the Corvette's low hood profile.

There were other modifications demanded by the Styling priority of keeping the hood neat and low. The rocker box cover was flattened at the front, and the oil filler was moved to the back. The final adjustment in favor of greater power was a dual exhaust system. The Corvette six then produced more than 150bhp at 4500 rpm. The standard 235-inch engine's output was 105bhp, so the new sportster's unit, which was of course stunningly chromed for its Motorama appearance, gave the whole project an air of competitive respectability. Less impressive to sports enthusiasts was the use of Chevrolet's Powerglide two-speed automatic transmission, but Olley and Cole simply ran out of time. Chevrolet had no suitable manual box, and there was no obvious way of modifying what they did have.

For all that, the Motorama Corvette was a sensational success. It undoubtedly stole the show, and the immediate response suggested that everyone from Harley Earl to Tom Keating had been absolutely right: America wanted a sports car.

CHAPTER 2

1953-1956: FROM CRUISER TO RACER

The decision to put the Corvette into production was not the result of a hot-tempered drawn-out classic boardroom confrontation. After the Motorama it was a foregone conclusion that it would go into production. However, these were early days for the Corvette, and the way in which the corporation behaved did reflect a lack of conviction on the part of some of the individuals involved. The corporate uncertainty was amply demonstrated in the length of the first Corvette run: a mere 300.

The car itself was ambivalent. Some of its compromised engineering was the result of shortage of time and appropriate raw materials; but some of it was the result of the corporation's wish to hedge its bets. Sales person supreme Keating, for example, argued that the Corvette should stay firmly in touch with those buyers, however young or old, who wanted a boulevard cruiser, and wanted with it a certain amount of comfort. Some argued that, in this context, the two-speed automatic transmission was perfect. After all, who really knew how to use a snappy four-speed crash box?

This understandable ambivalence might not have done the car any lasting harm, but the subsequent approach of its manufacturer to marketing almost killed it stone dead. The short run was also understandable, in its way. There was no fancy tooling as yet for fast assembly of GRP components, and initially the body sections were being molded by the Molded Fiber Glass Company in Ashtabula, Ohio, and shipped to GM's Flint, Michigan, plant for assembly. The public, on mere sight of the car at Motoramas, or even reports of Motoramas, had expressed written interest through their dealers. Apparently, America wanted at least 20,000 Corvettes.

Obviously, Chevrolet could not meet that sort of demand, or anything like it. Anxious not to lose the momentum, its sales team were instructed to sell the first 300 to loosely-termed 'celebrities.' It was a promotional ploy that fell flat. By the end of the 1953 production run, short as it was, less than 200 Corvettes had been sold.

This may have been because of the peculiarly poor advertising and publicity arrangements made for the Corvette. For some reason, GM departed from the normal practice of making test models available to the press in time to co-ordinate with its various lead times, and made no cars available until September 1953. No road tests appeared until Christmas, and it was almost another year before advertisements for the car began to appear in the motoring press. It is easy to understand that Chevrolet did not want to stimulate a demand it could not meet, but the Motorama Corvette had already done just that. By failing to go through the normal publicity routine, GM appeared to have undermined the support it needed for the few cars it had produced.

The tests, when they did appear, were on the whole enthusiastic and encouraging. However, by that time, the Corvette appeared to be falling pretty firmly between the two stools so carefully arranged for it by GM's initial uncertainties. The cruise-in-comfort crowd found fault in the car's unacceptable hard edges, and the fast set thought it was too slow and too soft.

Chevrolet, now, took a long time to react. Production had been moved to St Louis, Missouri, and improved, while MFG was now able to supply body components at a very impressive rate – the 1954 maximum was 50 cars a day – but still the corporation had found no way of connecting up with what remained of the 20,000 Corvette enthusiasts. It struggled on with the VIP policy until the middle of 1954, at which point it decided to cut back on production. About 3600 cars were made in 1954, and at the end of that year there were at least 1000 unsold. It began to occur to General Motors that it had made a mistake. Between the euphoria of the Motorama reception and the appalling sales figures of 1954, something had gone wrong with the Corvette.

There were, as it happened, a couple of major elements missing from the union of the two automotive traditions. One was the presence in the project of a dominant racer-engineer, and the other was that indispensable high-octane ingredient, competition with Ford. Luckily for the Corvette, it was in 1955

Right: The 1955 Motorama Corvette, with roll-up windows and stylish hard top, signaled GM's concern for comfort.

that the Ford Motor Company announced the Thunderbird.

The T-bird was not really a sports car, but it looked like one. Ford was not willing to chance its arm in such an unpredictable market so it carefully referred to the Thunderbird as a two-seater 'personal' car. Aware that it would not be as fast as the six-cylinder Corvette, Ford discreetly declined to tango. But still, it was all General Motors needed. Ford may not have aimed at the sports-car market, but if the Corvette were to fold, it would get a large piece of it anyway. Not only that, but Ford was well tooled-up for the Thunderbird and able to produce substantial numbers of the new car right away, which infuriated General Motors.

Even so, GM might not have been able to breathe any new life into the Corvette had it not been for the timely emergence, in 1955, of the new Chevrolet V8 engine. The V8 changed the image of the Corvette practically overnight and left the boulevard, once and for all, to Ford and their Thunderbird. From then on, the Corvette became a racer. As it happened, the other missing element in the development of the American sports car emerged during the course of 1955: an engineer-racer in the very best tradition, Zora Arkus-Duntov.

At first, the V8 was offered as an alternative to the six, but it turned out to be by far the more popular choice, which was a strong indicator to GM about the sports-car market's taste. The engine had been in development for some time, and

although it was intended for use in a number of Chevrolet models, the impulse behind it was the same one that gave birth to the Corvette: the need to speed up the sagging image of Chevrolet.

The new engine was light and powerful. The castings themselves were unusually thin, the valve gear and the crankshaft itself were lightweight, and a very short stroke gave the motor a very high-revving nature. Ed Cole had inherited the project when he took over as chief engineer, and the V8 bore his stamp, particularly in the area of combustion and gas flow. Cole redesigned the chambers and enlarged the engine's capacity. The 265-cubic inch small-block certainly transformed the Corvette: its 0–60 mph (97 km/h) elapsed time dropped from more than 11 seconds to a mere eight and a half. Which made it just about as fast as the much-admired Jaguar XK120M.

However, the 1955 car was a long way from perfection. Nothing of importance had changed apart from the engine since 1953, and so the Corvette remained uncomfortable and draughty, and it still leaked through the detachable side-windows. The brakes faded from average to poor, something that was made worse, rather than better by the V8. Although Chevrolet was making strenuous efforts with both advertising and general publicity, it was still lagging behind in deciding exactly what the car was.

Previous page: The SR-2 was a classic collaboration between GM Styling and Engineering. Fuel-injected, it developed 310bhp, and won a number of competition honors.

Far left: The 1954 Corvette was essentially unchanged.

Left: Bucket seats and plenty of instruments meant the Corvette was a sports car; but the Powerglide transmission still deterred some purists.

Far left: The barred grille was part of the aggressive side of the early Corvette's split personality.

Center: Glass reinforced plastic made for interesting styling.

Left: The roadster reveled in its new colors.

Below: Cascade Green, one of the new colors for 1954, was part of Styling's holding operation.

Maybe the public still thought of it as a boulevardier, in which case it was in terminal trouble. The other boulevard contender, the Ford Thunderbird, wiped the floor with the Corvette. Ford cheerfully sold more than 16,000 of the new two-seaters; Chevrolet made just 700 Corvettes in 1955, and it seemed that the public clamor for Corvettes had died. GM's whole approach to the marketing of the Corvette had been a masterpiece of ineptitude.

In May 1953 Zora Arkus-Duntov joined the General Motors Research and Development department. He had already had an interesting career in automotive engineering, and it is easy to see him now as the spirited representative of the great tradition of Louis Chevrolet. Like Louis, he was by birth a European (his parents were Russian, though he was born in Belgium and educated in Germany), and like Louis, he had a passion for racing. He was racing while he worked for Sydney Allard in England (while there he designed his renowned Ardun head for the flathead Ford V8) and he was still racing in his early days at GM. Duntov won his class at Le Mans in both 1954 and 1955. While he was at Allard he wrote to Ed Cole with a view to landing a job with GM. GM's response was negative until Duntov sent Cole some of his work on high-performance engines; Maurice Olley read it, and gave him a desk at R&D without further ado. One of the first things he did, out of professional interest rather than necessity, was to take an early Corvette to the proving ground.

Duntov was half-impressed. The Corvette, in his considered view, had great potential, but had steering and stopping problems. The front end oversteered, and the back end understeered, but Duntov managed to cure both after relatively minor adjustments to springing and stabilizing, and thus established, at least within GM, that the Corvette did indeed have race-track potential.

Duntov became more closely involved with the Corvette when Olley asked him to find out why the exhausts were fouling the paintwork at the rear of the car, as well as making their presence smelt inside the passenger compartment. Intelligent observation of airflow revealed that opening the ventilator so radically interfered with the aerodynamic qualities of the body, that the air, in some critical areas, actually flowed backward. The solution was the relatively straightforward one of locating the tailpipes at the end of each of the rear fenders, so that the gases were unaffected by the adverse flow.

The arrival of Zora Arkus-Duntov at GM coincided with both the appearance of the Corvette and the decision to produce the V8 engine for forthcoming Chevrolets. It was too late for him to become involved with the first-model Corvette in any very fundamental way, but it was inevitable, particularly after his impressive work for Olley, that he should be drawn into the plans for the second generation, which began with model year 1956. That the '56 was the first of the true racing Corvettes is a simple reflection of the fact that Duntov was involved.

His first contribution was in the area of handling. Typically, he did the preliminary testing himself: in a 1955 prototype equipped with a V8 engine, he set about finding ways of securing greater high-speed stability, a more consistent steering response at all speeds, and of getting maximum power on to the road during cornering. Again, though tests were complex, the solutions were decisive and straightforward. The rake geometry of the front end was modified, and at the rear, the springs were rehung to correct roll understeer. The front end was also relieved of troublesome understeer. The stock 1956 Corvette appeared with steering sufficiently neutral to make it a serious contender in national sports-car racing.

Of course, what the public saw in January 1956 was not revised suspension geometry, but revised styling. The new look for '56, which was handsome, sleek, and somehow just plain fast, was the perfect complement to the car's new per-

Left: At 195bhp, the new V8 was a godsend for the Corvette.

Above right: The 1954 emphasized the styling principles of Harley Earl.

formance potential. Certainly it made the Thunderbird look like some sort of gaily-painted military patrol vehicle, though there is no doubt that the new Corvette's concessions to passenger comfort – draught-free roll-up windows, for example – were made with the Ford in mind.

The '56 was the child of three major styling influences. Two GM Motorama cars, the LaSalle and the Biscayne, featured boldly, indeed heavily-grilled front ends and long scoops in the bodywork, running backward and forward, respectively, from their wheel arches. Both cars displayed a nice concern for color keying, both inside and outside. The Corvette appeared with the long concave body feature, running back from the wheel almost to the rear of the door, and, making use of the scoop, it offered a new range and combinations of colors. Its other obvious influence was the Mercedes 300SL. The Corvette came out with curved, styled, and slightly thrusting front fenders, and two parallel ridges raised in the hood. But for all that, it was an extremely fresh-looking car, neater by far than either of the GM show cars, and giving nothing away to the Mercedes in terms of the classic speedster's lines.

The V8 was also suitably tweaked for the occasion. A new cylinder head produced a new compression ratio of 9.5:1; larger-capacity exhaust manifolds were introduced, along with stronger exhaust valves and new heat-dispersing aluminum rocker-box covers. More reliable ignition was provided by a twin-breaker distributor. The use of a single Carter carburetor with a cast-iron inlet manifold produced a stock 210bhp at 5200 rpm; the twin four-barrel option with an aluminum manifold turned in no less than 225bhp. Transmission was a standard three-speed manual box, with Powerglide offered as an option. The fact that the Corvette was offered with optional axle ratios was perhaps the final confirmation that Chevrolet meant business – on the racetrack, as well as on the road.

While all this was going on, Ed Cole dispatched Zora Duntov to GM's proving ground in Phoenix, Arizona with an elderly V8 bolted into a 1954 Corvette prototype chassis. There was a sporting event to be held in Daytona, Florida, in February, and Chevrolet wanted to be there.

Duntov's Phoenix tests were aimed at enabling him to calculate the precise power that would be needed for the 1956 Corvette to break the production car speed record at Daytona only weeks after its introduction to the public. It was an important step for Chevrolet: they were ready to sell their car on the basis of its performance in competition – something they had not done since the days of Louis Chevrolet. Not only were they going for the record, they also intended to race in the 1956 Daytona Speed Weeks sports-car events. There was a new spirit of resolution in the board room, and the alliance of Duntov and Cole appeared set to give Chevrolet an image it could barely have dreamed of since Billy Durant set up the company with the Chevrolet Brothers.

What Phoenix taught Duntov was that the V8 needed a new and hotter camshaft. He was looking at a deficit of about 30bhp, and there was no other realistic way of obtaining it. Duntov was confident that the already well-tried bottom end could handle the additional stress. There was a brief bureaucratic delay while the highly individualistic camshaft proposed by Duntov was approved, but when he got it back to Phoenix, he was more than satisfied with the result. The Corvette, which by now was beginning to resemble the dashing '56, was suddenly capable of more than 160 mph (258 km/h).

Wet sand is not the ideal surface for a high-speed run, because in optimum conditions some wheelspin is inevitable. Even so, Duntov astonished the NASCAR timers at Daytona

Far left: The SR-2 underlined GM's growing confidence in the Corvette.

Center: Daytona paint job said the Corvette meant business.

Left: Racing regulations called for a Plexi-glass bubble to cover the cockpit, seen here in cruising trim.

Below: Big and heavy, the SR-2 was impressive, nonetheless, on the racetrack.

when he whipped up and down the beach for a two-way average of 150.58 mph (242.28 km/h).

When the official Speed Weeks began in February, General Motors faced Ford, head-on. In the lists were a number of factory-supported Thunderbirds, very much dressed for the occasion. Ford just held off the Corvette in the standing mile runs, but lost decisively in the top speed stakes. Adverse winds prevented Duntov from repeating his earlier performance, but he set a fast time of 147.30 mph (237 km/h). John Fitch recorded 145.54 mph (234.17 km/h) and Betty Skelton 137.77 mph (221.56 km/h). Ed Cole and GM were encouraged and the next step was obviously to try road racing. A full factory team of four cars was entered (albeit under the auspices of Dick Doane's Raceway Enterprises) for the 12 Hours of Sebring, on 24 March. Fitch was hired as team manager, and given almost five weeks to get ready.

There had, of course, been some private, rather tentative racing of Corvettes before the factory made its decision, and GM undoubtedly knew that a V8 '55 had turned in respectable performances against imported cars in production sports events, and had demolished their share of Thunderbirds. Not only that, but a certain Zora Arkus-Duntov had set a new class record in the Pikes Peak hill climbs.

Chevrolet team engineers had also taken the trouble to run a few laps with the Corvette at Sebring during the Daytona episode, but other than that, they were racing blind. They really did not know what would happen, and a good deal of board-room prestige, if nothing else, was committed to a small bunch of race technicians in a small shed on the perimeter of an obscure Florida airfield. These were heady times indeed.

Sebring was not an out-and-out success but neither was it a disaster. Viewed objectively, it could have been described as 'useful.' But nobody at GM, least of all Ed Cole and Zora Duntov, was interested in looking at it that way. They were all too heavily committed to rescuing the Corvette, and the prestige the corporation had thus far invested.

The weeks of preparation at Sebring had given the Chevy engineers a great deal of valuable information about the Corvette, not least in the area of brakes. But more important was that the race itself provided a result. The first two cars caved in during the early stages, Fitch brought an overbored class B car limping home ninth, and the last car, driven by Ray Crawford and Max Goldman exclusively in top gear for most of the race, finished 15th. That was not bad and it gave GM's advertising staff their first real chance to crow about Chevrolet's high-performance car. And with it, Chevrolet's new high-octane image.

The famous ad, which showed an urgent refueling of a lean, stripped-looking Corvette, made a simple but telling claim for the car. 'The Real McCoy,' said the headline. Although Chevrolet were unabashedly selling cars on the strength of racing, they made a lengthy point of just how luxurious this 'torpedo-on-wheels with the stamina to last through the brutal 12 hours of Sebring' really was. Whatever you had heard about leaking windows, forget it.

The Real McCoy ad came in support of one drawing attention to Betty Skelton's Daytona record. The copy also said that 'Corvette owners may enter other big racing tests in the months ahead — tests that may carry America's blue-and-white colors into several of the most important European competitions.' It must have seemed at the time that there was just no end to Chevrolet's new-found confidence and the headline proclaimed 'Bring on the hay bales!'

After the modest success of Sebring, Zora Duntov was beginning to plan for the 24 Hours of Le Mans, but in the meantime, he immediately had what had been learned in Florida built into a car for the Sports Car Club of America's Class C Production championship. The driver was already selected, one Richard Thompson, an extremely fast dentist from Washington, DC.

Thompson was well known for his SCCA successes with Jaguars, though he had driven a Corvette as early as 1954,

Right: The '56 suddenly made the first Corvette look almost stately.

Right: Hedging their bets took GM as far as the Nomad experimental station wagon.

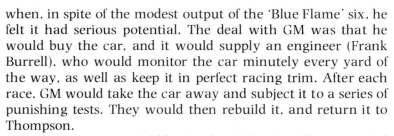

when, in spite of the modest output of the 'Blue Flame' six, he felt it had serious potential. The deal with GM was that he would buy the car, and it would supply an engineer (Frank Burrell), who would monitor the car minutely every yard of the way, as well as keep it in perfect racing trim. After each race, GM would take the car away and subject it to a series of punishing tests. They would then rebuild it, and return it to Thompson.

First time out, at Pebble Beach, California, Thompson led the race until his brakes began to fail. He finished second overall, but won his class. Chevy's ad recalling that auspicious

The 1956 brought the body-scoops that endured to 1962. The '56 was longer, narrower, a little heavier, but more powerful.

occasion went all the way, addressing itself to the 'competition driver,' and telling the others that the Corvette was indeed 'America's only genuine production sports car.'

Thompson continued to drive well, the Corvette continued to be both fast and reliable, and they won the championship. This time, it was not just a matter of what the advertisements said. Much more to the point was that Ed Cole and his team appeared to have justified the decision to go racing. They had learned an amazing amount that could be directly and immediately applied to the production cars, and they had already given the Corvette the hardest, most certain image in the whole of the American auto industry.

Racing had become respectable at GM. Halfway through 1956, Duntov had already embarked on another interesting project, aimed in part at Sebring the following year. Even so, the racing and the excitement it generated were shrouding the real news of 1956: the 1957 Corvette. Racing was of great interest to Duntov, and of measurable value to GM, but it was not what he had been employed for. Since 1955, he had been working with John Dolza's power development team on fuel injection. Edward N Cole was among those who wanted to see the whole rather sluggish business of injection development speeded up, and the bureaucracy surrounding it whittled down. What he wanted in particular was to see fuel injection offered as an option for the 1957 Corvette.

In July of 1956, Ed Cole became the general manager of the Chevrolet Division of General Motors. That did not mean, in itself, that he could do exactly what he wanted. It meant that those who wanted and believed in the American sports car were in key positions in the American industry. Soon Zora Arkus-Duntov would become the Corvette's chief engineer, and an energetically imaginative man by the name of Bill Mitchell would become GM's chief stylist. In a matter of a very few years, the sports car had moved, in spirit, if not in numbers sold, to the center of the automotive stage. The Corvette was here to stay.

1957: BRING ON THE HAY BALES!

If ever a car manufacturer came out fighting, it was Chevrolet, with the 1957 Corvette. First, it was offered with fuel-injected engine, which was the first offer of its kind in American automotive history. Second, the fuel-injected option could turn out one brake horsepower for every one of its 283 cu in of displacement. Which was another first for the American mass-produced motor car.

Furthermore, within a couple of months of its launch, the Corvette of '57 was available with a four-speed manual gearbox. Also offered as an option was a 4.11:1 rear axle. The hottest combination of these offers from Chevrolet would take a Corvette from 0–60 mph (97 km/h) in 5.7 seconds. Still not a real sports car? Well, sir, why not try the RPO 684 handling option? Heavier springs all round, larger volume

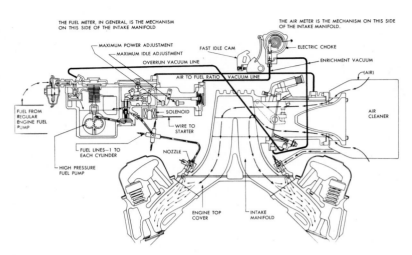

Above: The stunning power of the '57 Corvette derived from its fuel injection system, the first to be offered in a production car.

Left: Red was the perfect color for the new fire-breather.

Below: By 1957 interior styling changes were somewhat overdue.

Right: John Fitch with Zora Arkus-Duntov's SS at Sebring in 1957. The Corvette's early racing history was very encouraging for GM.

Previous page: The 1957 Corvette looked terrific and went like a rocket. It displaced 283 cubic inches, and delivered 283bhp – an American first.

shock absorbers, an anti-sway bar at the front, heavy-duty brakes of the kind developed for Sebring, limited slip differential, and a quick steering adaptor. Please choose one of three possible axle ratios.

By the summer of 1957 it was possible to drive away from the showroom a Corvette that looked good, went unbelievably fast, steered well, and stopped — presentably well. What you could buy was a Corvette ready to race, and ready, if you were, to win.

Chevrolet's decision to make a fuel-injection engine was made at a time when the very idea was exciting and everybody had an opinion about it. Most people knew that it had its merits in racing, because racing did not call for such street-going necessities as a smooth idle. Most people around Detroit knew that a good fuel-injection system for street cars could be built in America, at a price. Nobody knew whether some system could be devised to make a fuel-injection car a realistic proposition for the average American car buyer. Well, nobody knew for certain, but Chevrolet thought they knew. So it was hardly surprising that the work they began in 1955 was done in the utmost secrecy. The success of the V8, particularly in competition, was a useful smokescreen. With the kind of power already available, why would Chevy be meddling with something like fuel injection?

Chevrolet certainly was power-minded, but injection was not regarded as a matter of power. Its attraction was primarily that it was the most efficient way of getting fuel into the combustion chamber. As such it should logically have led to better fuel consumption, better combustion, and more efficient use of the entire engine. That this was not the case was probably more the fault of sporty engineers and market forces than the idea itself. Certainly, by the time Chevy had finished developing its unit in conjunction with the Rochester Carburetor Division, its main virtue was seen as the stunning power it could produce.

The Chevrolet-Rochester system was such that the power produced was both consistent and flexible (when the unit was working normally, which, regrettably, was not always the case) and, to the surprise of the industry as well as the public, relatively inexpensive to produce, although the price of $481 only brought forward 240 buyers. Critical to the performance of any injection system is the way in which it detects the precise needs of the engine at any given speed. Chevy's unit got round the problem that had caused, for

example, Mercedes Benz such complicated headaches by locating a metering diaphragm across a large venturi, where it could detect pressure changes in the air flowing to the plenum chamber. The advantage of the system was that the diaphragm could control the amount of fuel reaching the nozzles without reference either to engine speed or the throttle control position.

As it turned out, carburetor engines were more than fast enough for most Corvette buyers in 1957. Chevrolet offered three carburetor models of the new 283 motors (achieved by boring about 1/8 inch out of the 265 barrels, thus adding to its oversquare nature and its tendency to rev hard), from a 220bhp unit, through 245bhp (twin four-barrel Carters and hydraulic lifters) to a 270bhp rascal with twin fours and hot Duntov camshaft. There were two injection engines, the base unit at a mere 250bhp, while the fast one reached the fabled 283bhp courtesy of a Duntov camshaft and a compression ratio of 10.5:1. In addition there was option RPO 579E, provided for those who were interested in racing. Its main appeal was a cold air intake for the injection system.

Now all this was really quite comprehensive, from the point of view of the sports-car fan. At the end of 1952, there simply was no General Motors sports car, that is no American sports car, to speak of. A little over four years later, there was, well, the 1957 Corvette, a handsome, blisteringly fast sports car featuring the most advanced production engine in the world.

The year 1957 was significant in a number of other ways. In addition to being the year in which the Corvette really took off, it was the year in which it received a real setback. The Automobile Manufacturers Association decided, partially because it was anxious not to attract repressive legislation, to recommend that its members should cease all racing activities and stop using racing in their advertising campaigns. Ironically for the Corvette, it was GM's president, Harlow Curtice, who made the proposal.

Corvette development began to break off in different directions. The project begun by Zora Arkus-Duntov in mid-1956 was intended to produce a Corvette-type racing sports car that would lead to Chevrolet's not merely attending the races, but dominating them. This car, which was light, nimble, and developed over 300bhp, became known as the Corvette SS.

Duntov was the engineer for the project, and Clare Mac-Kichan was responsible for styling. Urging the team along was none other than Chevrolet's general manager, Ed Cole. What

Left: In 1958 the Corvette grew from 168 inches to 177.2, fattening out to 72.8 inches. Weight was up from 2880 to 3080lbs.

Above: The '58 took on some chrome, but its standard output was up from 220bhp at 4800rpm to 245 at 5000. The Corvette was still a very fast car.

Cole wanted was for the SS to go to Sebring in 1957 and blow the Ferraris and Jaguars into the weeds. However, he was unable to give much of his valuable attention to the project and Duntov went into 1957 with just two cars: one the SS itself, and the other a test-bed cobbled together out of extra panels and spare parts that Duntov called his 'Mule.' The Mule played some part in the events at Sebring, for there it was taken out during practice sessions by both Stirling Moss and Juan Manuel Fangio, under whose direction it turned in one of the best times set in the practice session. It would eventually play a much more important role in the history of the Corvette.

The SS proper, looking at least a million dollars ($1,500,000 was nearer the mark) was insufficiently tested at Sebring, and Piero Taruffi, who had flown from Italy for the race, surrendered after just over an hour to a worn bushing in the rear suspension. The day was by no means lost, however, since stock '57 Corvettes went on to finish 12th (Richard Thompson) and 15th. In 16th place was another Corvette special, the SR-2, which had been built by GM's styling staff essentially as a show car, but, in keeping with the spirit of the times, a show car that could be raced.

The Mule had impressed in practice (as well it might have, since it positively glowed with engineering innovation), and the Thompson/Andrey car had won its class. Cole and Duntov really were, just as the advertisement said, planning to take the fight to the Europeans. Sebring had been a try-out for Le Mans, and as far as our dedicated pair of racers were concerned, the car had proved its worth. Cole went back to Detroit, and Duntov was taking a few days off in Florida when news reached him of the AMA ban on motor racing.

Of course, there was more racing for a while, because things took a little time to wind down, and while that was happening, racers were making other arrangements. Dick Thompson's Corvette went on to win the SCCA B championship, and the Corvette was now firmly established as a racing car. It would be a long time before Washington and Detroit between them would be able to persuade the American public otherwise.

CHAPTER 4

1958-1962: THE AMERICAN SPORTS CAR MATURES

The trim, purposeful lines of the 1956 and 1957 Corvettes suddenly gave way in 1958 to a messy and slightly ponderous-looking body. The change had nothing to do with the AMA racing decision, though the public drew the obvious and mistaken conclusion that GM was suddenly trying to look respectable, after so spectacularly letting its hair down in 1957.

The look of the new Corvette was indeed respectable, but what it reflected was not remorse but compromise born of conflict in GM generally about what was the function of the car. One faction won out in 1957, another in 1958. The idea was that the '58 model should somehow suggest refinement, comfort and luxury, without actually looking sluggish. To this end, a range of irritating embellishments was added onto the once clean-cut body. Two headlights appeared on either side of a toothy but weighty-looking grille, and each of them had an elongated hump running back along the fender. Between the humps was a chrome strip. The humps were emphasized by two ribs running along the hood, while between the ribs were 18 ridges, no doubt intended to look like louvers.

The profile of the car was largely retained from 1956–57, but it too suffered from the addition of superfluous chrome. The interior, including the instruments, was reworked, and, on the whole, improved. But even so, Styling had failed to get a grip on the aesthetics of the cockpit area. However this apparent muddle was quite deliberate. GM was trying to make the Corvette look glamorous. At that particular moment, glamorous meant big, and Styling had simply given in, gone

along with it. The idea was that some of the glamor would rub off on the whole Chevrolet range. After all, the Corvette had already proved that it could go fast. The time had come, felt GM, for a little visual swagger. Taste apart, they may have been right. Chevrolet built 9168 units in 1958, against 6339 for 1957, and 3467 for 1956.

The Corvette certainly faced both ways in terms of power. The leading engine option of 1958 was RPO 579D, a 283 V8 with improved fuel injection and an output of 290bhp. So, in spite of the stern official disapproval of racing and all that went with it, the Corvette was more powerful (and, in spite of the extra weight, every bit as fast). On the other hand, one of the carburetor engines on offer turned out a mere 230bhp. It still added up to a fast motor car, but Chevrolet was evidently anxious to demonstrate, with at least one of the options, that it had not turned its back forever on the boulevard cruisers of America.

However, there was far too much impetus behind the Corvette's racing career for it to be stopped short by a mere committee decision, however lofty. The '57 had unleashed a beast that kept on running in '58, and for years to come. Inevitably, there were Corvettes at Sebring, and one of them (which, this time, really was entered, and driven, by Dick Doane, along with Jim Rathmann) won the GT class. An advertising man called Jim Jeffords won the SCCA B production championship in a car sometimes called 'The Purple People Eater.' This car was a Corvette SR-2, and it belonged to Bill Mitchell, who was shortly to become a very influential head of GM Styling. Mitchell's freelance racing enterprise was

Previous page: The body-scoops provided plenty of opportunity for drama in color and chrome.

Below left: The '58 looked toward the cruising market, but its injected engine turned out 290bhp.

Right: The Corvette came with a shopping option engine in 1958 — producing a mere 230bhp.

Following page, main picture: The influence of Harley Earl was still evident in 1960.

Following page, top left: The '60, in red and white.

Following page, top right: The 1960 cockpit was a touch tidier.

by no means out of the ordinary for senior GM staff. Zora Duntov had already begun throwing his weight into certain NASCAR projects, and it was not long before he began building his CERV I racer.

Meanwhile, during the summer of 1958, Mitchell had been at work on a new styling-exercise show car, designated the XP-700. Evident in the car were lines that were soon to become very familiar to sports-car enthusiasts. It is interesting to note, in 1958, what Bill Mitchell's priorities were. He seemed to take it entirely for granted that racing and styling went hand in hand.

In 1959, the Corvette shed some of its trim (notably the false hood louvers) and received some welcome attention to detail. The interior was tidied up, and a gear-shift lever that locked out reverse was installed. The wheel trims were modified to allow more air through to the drums, and sintered metallic linings were offered as an option for the first time.

The most significant improvement of 1959, however, was the addition by Duntov of radius rods located between the rear side frame members and the axle housing. The rods were pivoted and moved up and down, but they canceled the torque reaction twisting of the axle housing and consequently relieved the springs of torque effect. The aim of this operation was to stop the back end hopping under acceleration, and it was largely successful. However, Duntov was among those who felt that the suspension of the Corvette still left a lot to be desired.

The following model year gave him further opportunities for improvements. He fitted an anti-roll bar to the rear, which allowed for softer springing, even for racers, and he increased the strength of the front stabilizer. The upshot was that the 1960 Corvette kept a much more even keel, hard cornering notwithstanding.

Duntov also chopped some weight off the 1960 model by

introducing an aluminum clutch housing, which saved all of 18 lbs. Also introduced as an option was a light-weight aluminum radiator. Aluminum was also a theme in the engine department, where Duntov upped the output of the 283 to 315bhp. Increased compression ratio (11:1) and a larger-volume plenum chamber were mainly responsible, but Duntov added aluminum cylinder heads, in the interests of saving weight. As it turned out, they were prone to warping, and were soon dropped.

There was still a racing option for the Corvette, and it could hardly have escaped the general notice that Corvettes were still racing, even though the factory had turned its back on racing. Jim Jeffords again won the SCCA B production championship in 1959, this time with a stock Corvette, and in 1960, Briggs Cunningham took a team of Corvettes to Le Mans. It may not have been a factory team, but it was certainly the descendant of one. Ed Cole and Zora Arkus-Duntov were no doubt extremely gratified when John Fitch and Bob Grossman brought their GT class car home eighth. It was a symbolic achievement for the American sports car, and, without doubt, the Europeans were impressed.

The year 1961 was the first in which Bill Mitchell's influence became evident in the Corvette's styling. There was nothing very radical about it to begin with — just a jaunty little flick of the tail. Mitchell underlined the rather rich curve of the rear fender with a sharp rib running back from the wheel arch. The trunk lid was flattened out slightly, and the bottom rear panel was swept quite severely up to meet the end of the rib. It was a clean, interesting stroke, reminiscent of the 1958 XP-700, and it suggested brisk styling changes to come.

Elsewhere, there were detail changes. The circular emblem at the nose was dropped in favor of an unadorned crossed flag motif, and immediately below it appeared a simple grid in place of the barred grille, which, along with the wraparound windshield and the fake knock-off wheels, was all that re-

Right: The 1960 Corvette, in Honduras Maroon.

Left: In 1960 the XP-700 experimental car gave away a good deal of what Styling were thinking.

Right: In 1961 the first signs of Bill Mitchell's influence on the Corvette were visible.

Left: GM, whatever the official policy, was never far from the racetrack. Zora Arkus-Duntov's CERV I.

Left: The 1960 Corvette reflected a resurgence of GM's uncertainty about the sports-car market.

mained of the styling of the 1953 curtain-raiser. Engines and suspension remained much the same.

The 1962 car was neater yet. Mitchell had de-emphasized the body scoops by removing their chrome trim and substituting a small grille for the three horizontal chrome ribs behind the wheel arch. While Bill Mitchell was making his general intentions plain enough with the exterior of the Corvette, a significant management change had taken place at Chevrolet. Ed Cole, on his way to becoming president of General Motors, had vacated the general managership of Chevrolet in favor of Semon E 'Bunkie' Knudsen. Knudsen liked the Corvette (indeed, he liked it so much that he asked Zora Arkus-Duntov to build 100 special racing models, known as the Corvette GS) but he was less interested in racing it than selling it.

Ever since Corvette production had moved to St Louis in 1954, output had somehow rather lamely trailed demand. Knudsen thought it was about time that production of what had become a very sophisticated and saleable car was stepped up. Supply of body parts from Ashtabula was by now both efficient and predictable, and so shortly after the 1962 model run began, Knudsen ordered a second shift to start work. In 1961 Chevrolet had sold 10,939 Corvettes; in 1962 they produced 14,531. The Corvette was still a low-volume car; but at least it was no longer a production-line embarrassment.

CHAPTER 5

1963-1967: THE STING RAY

The development of a car that becomes a classic is not as conveniently linear as its historians would perhaps like it to be. We have already noted that between 1956 and 1957 the story of the Corvette began to go in different directions, and in order to understand the styling and engineering developments of 1963, we have to go back to that day early in 1957 when news came through to Florida that the major manufacturers, including GM, were backing out of racing.

Some of the hardware involved was sold, and some things, like the Corvette SS itself, were used as exhibits. There was no way, on the other hand, that the development work put into these vehicles could be recouped so easily: it would have to emerge in its own way in the development of subsequent road models.

There was likely to be a particular problem with Zora Duntov's test bed, his SS Mule. It no longer had any kind of function, and yet what a crime to junk it. Fangio had driven it, and Moss, and it had accumulated an amazing amount of automotive knowledge. The real SS, by comparison, was nothing more than a pretender. Moss had been very rude about the Mule's appearance, a sort of racing slum, a 'bucket of bolts' and he had teased Duntov about it. But it was an impressive car, and it would have become a formidable racer.

For all that, the Mule was hauled back to Detroit, and there it stayed for a year, under the steady and thoughtful gaze of a racing enthusiast and GM stylist called William L Mitchell. Happily for Mitchell, the Mule chassis fell into the apparently harmless hands of Styling soon after it arrived home. When the racing furore had died down somewhat, Mitchell sent GM a long memo, arguing as powerfully as he knew how the advantages to the corporation of his being allowed to build a racing car on the Mule chassis and to race it, privately.

Mitchell got permission, though with misgivings, grumbles, and even, in some places, outrage. So, in the 1959 season, Bill Mitchell became the owner of a racing car and in the

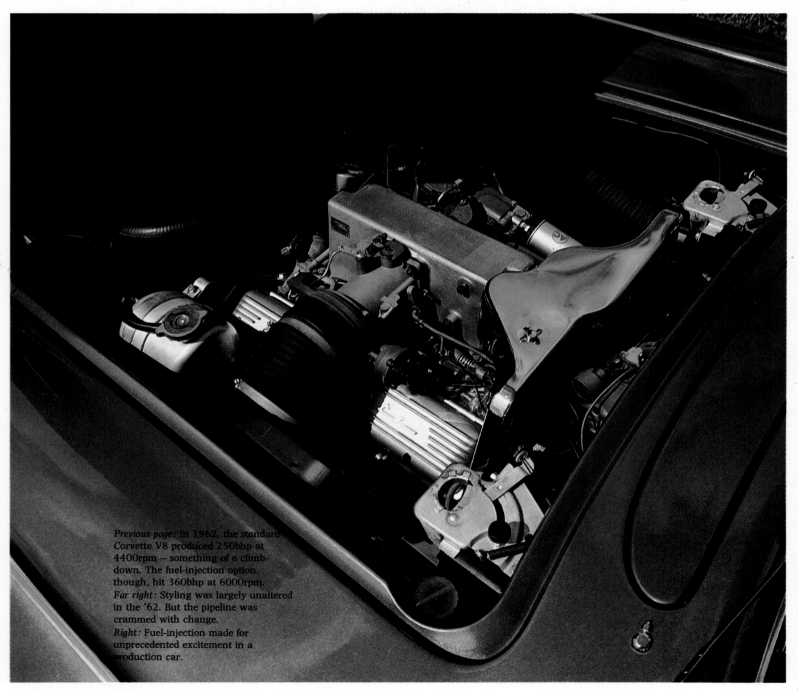

Previous page: In 1962, the standard Corvette V8 produced 250bhp at 4400rpm — something of a climb-down. The fuel-injection option, though, hit 360bhp at 6000rpm.
Far right: Styling was largely unaltered in the '62. But the pipeline was crammed with change.
Right: Fuel-injection made for unprecedented excitement in a production car.

The Chevrolet Sting Ray was an epoch-making automobile. Fuel-injection, 360bhp, and a highly-developed V8 made for speed and reliability.

Right: Flip-up headlamps were the perfect complement to the Sting Ray's aggressive lines.

Below: The Sting Ray lost its split rear window in 1964, but retained its dramatic outline.

Below right: The '64 in Silver-blue.

process of producing his one-off racer, Mitchell gave body to one of the most exciting styling exercises ever to emerge from the US automotive industry. More than an exercise, the revived Mule was to set a tone that not only changed attitudes in Detroit, but set a new status for American stylists in the eyes of the rest of the world. Mitchell called his new car the Sting Ray.

Fresh as it was, the Sting Ray was still part of the Corvette tradition. Mitchell asked stylist Larry Shinoda to develop the thinking behind the Q-Corvette, a design worked up in 1957 for the 1960 Corvette. Bob McLean had been in charge of the Q project, and he in turn had been working on Mitchell's suggestion that they might be able to make something of the early Boano and Pininfarina themes centered on strong horizontal lines softened by curving at the wheels and on the upper body.

The styling team succeeded quite spectacularly. The Q-Corvette's clean, fast, slim elegance would have looked sparklingly good 20 years later. GM senior decision makers were impressed. It was cleared for production, even though it was likely to be expensive, but unfortunately 1958 was a poor year for the industry in general and cutbacks were made. The Q-Corvette was canceled, and 1960 turned out to be just another year.

Shinoda's Sting Ray sported the strongest possible horizontal motif. From a long nose above a functional, almost insignificant grille, the car's meridian cut straight back to an equally decisive tail, throwing the bottom half of the car into a highly dramatic penumbra. The Sting Ray turned heads for miles around, and for years to come.

The engine was a hot 283 V8 that got steadily hotter during the two years that the car raced. During 1959, Dick Thompson, and later, John Fitch (Thompson had to sit out a 90-day suspension for over-enthusiasm) drove the car to good effect, and Mitchell and his team learned a lot about racing a special. For 1960, the car was lighter, and used stiffer springs. It was painted a still more dramatic metallic silver. Halfway through the season, Thompson had clinched the C modified SCCA championship.

Officially, no one was supposed to know what, exactly, the Sting Ray was. Around the tracks, it was billed simply as 'Sting Ray,' and there was, of course, no mention of Chevrolet. No one could perhaps be expected to ascertain the origins of its chassis, but the Sting Ray was obviously Chevrolet, from the identity of its owner, to those of its drivers, Corvette aces both. When, in 1961, Chevrolet reclaimed the Sting Ray, stuck emblems on it, and sent it forth as a show car, no one was very surprised.

Mitchell may not have been acting in the name of GM, but he was at least given plenty of support by General Motors. Bill Mitchell was part of GM, and the corporation was finding a way to allow itself to be imaginative, creative, even outrageous. It was finding a way through the corporate caution, the narrow mindedness, the red tape, and the financial necessities that naturally govern its behavior. GM may or may not have known what it was doing, but it was GM, as much as Bill Mitchell, that built the Sting Ray. Above all, it was a remarkable exercise in economy, creative and corporate, since, at a stroke, the genius that went into the Q-Corvette, the SS Mule, and the SR-2, was saved, and amplified. GM, one way or another, had been smart.

The 1963 Chevrolet Corvette was called the Sting Ray. In many respects it was a whole new car. Certainly, it bore a far stronger resemblance to Mitchell's racer than to the 1962 Corvette. It featured a fiberglass body, but this was more for old times' sake than because it needed one. It also came equipped with one of the six Chevrolet engines available in the 1962 Corvette, but there the resemblance ended.

The chassis was different. Instead of the modified '53 X-member arrangement, there was a far stiffer ladder frame. There was a different front end, different and much better brakes, and, at the rear, there was independent suspension, derived largely from Zora Duntov's work with the CERV I experimental racer. The body, of course, was Mitchell's shapely interpretation of the themes of the Q-Corvette and his racing descendant of the SS.

The horizontal motif was very much in evidence, strongly supported by a dew-drop sweep from the windshield to the tail. The center line was strong from the nose, from where it ran between two dummy grilles taken straight from the racer, and so strong down the roof that it split the rear windshield in two, and public reaction to the styling of the car in much the same way. (Not only the public, Duntov hated it, because he felt it impaired rear visibility, and Mitchell insisted on it, saying that, without it, the project was worthless. Only behind-the-scenes diplomacy saved GM from an equally spectacular split of its own.)

The new car jolted the specialist press and somehow they found freshness and enthusiasm of their own to match the new product. The American magazines, in particularly, were wild about the Sting Ray, and a note that sounded like pride crept into their coverage. Here was an American sports car that needed no apology. The Europeans were again impressed, and generally took the arrival of this fast and sophisticated challenger in good part.

For all its roadholding and style, concealed headlights included, the Sting Ray was not without critics. The complaints were mainly in the area of finish and quality control. What had been pardonable at the start of the Corvette project, when the adventurous GM needed all the encouragement it

Left: To go racing, all you needed was a number plate.

Below: Class B Production was no place for easy pickings, but the Corvette triumphed.

could get, was unacceptable now that the Corvette was supposed to be one of the world's leading vehicles in its class. Testers also began pushing the car to new limits. After all, it was derived from a racer, but at the new limits, they began to find new faults. Expectations were rising as the Corvette improved. In a way it was flattering but in another way it was a warning. Chevrolet was in the big league with its performance car but maybe it should have had a look at the finish on a Mercedes.

GM seemed to take this into account. The outcry against Mitchell's handsome split window was such that it was dropped. So the '64 looked different. The fake louvers on the hood disappeared, and the ones behind the side windows became a functioning part of the ventilation system, which was much improved. Noise and vibration were measurably reduced by the use of stiffer panelling and sound proofing. Better silencers were employed and in order to improve on general ride qualities, variable-rate springing was introduced at both front and rear. The car was unquestionably improved and more comfortable, and the press again responded with enthusiasm.

The year 1965 saw further refinements, and further tidying up of the Sting Ray's styling, inside and outside. With refinement so very much in the air, Chevrolet even offered a steering wheel with adjustable reach. Again, the improvements, though small, were clear, and no one carped seriously. There

Far left: 1965 Corvette at the race-track – no finer setting.

Left: The 1966 Sting Ray equipped with 427 cubic inch engine. capable of delivering 425bhp at 6400rpm.

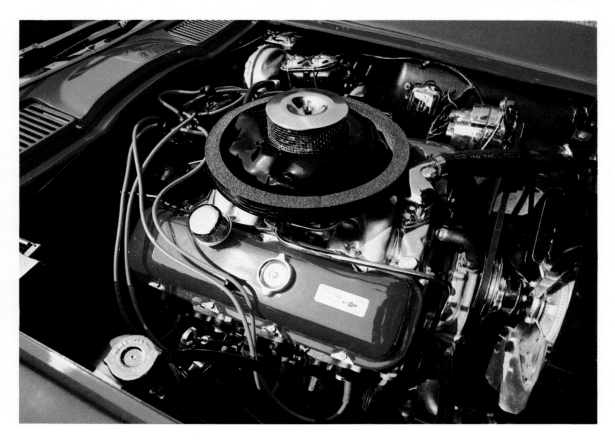

Far left: This 1967 Sting Ray featured the L88 racing option. 560bhp at 6400rpm was not everyone's idea of a toy.

Left: The L88 racing engine was available over the counter. But not for the fainthearted.

Previous page: The 1967 Corvette lived on borrowed time. The model that should have replaced it came a year late, in '68.

Right: The standard 427 cubic inch Mark IV engine offered in 1967 developed a useful 390bhp at 5400rpm.

Below: Buffed alloy side exhausts gave the '67 a menacing look.

was, however, big news in '65. First, the Sting Ray suddenly sported disk brakes on all four wheels, which produced relief all round. Early in the model year, Chevrolet announced an interesting new option: a 396-cu in carburetor V8 engine that delivered no less than 425bhp. Never did disk brakes seem to make more sense.

The engine made sense too. The 1960s were expansive times, and thus far neither the fear of pollution nor the oil crisis had cast their shadows. The fuel-injection Corvettes were fast, but there were others still faster. Carroll Shelby's AC Cobras, for example, were mauling the Corvettes in A production, and the GM engineers were naturally stung. So the Sting Ray got a big engine, and a chassis modified to match; 0–60 mph (97 km/h) dropped below 5 seconds. The big engine brought a style of its own — a menacing-looking bulge in the hood and the daring option of buffed-alloy side exhausts.

The new engine, the Mark IV, was entirely satisfactory. Fuel-injection was abandoned in 1966, but the Mark IV got bigger. Chevy, apparently still very sensitive to the speed of others, bored it out to 427cid. Not only that, but they offered a range of options from gearbox to suspension package and heavy duty brakes frankly intended for racing. The 1967 model was still more emphatic. Its hood sprouted a snarling scoop in frank acknowledgment of what was beneath, and Engineering came up with a new breathing system that added

significantly to the power available. If that were not enough, which it was, for most people, Chevy threw in a racing engine, the L88, with a compression ratio of 12.5:1 and an output of 560bhp. There seemed no end to it.

In many ways GM's behavior seemed almost irrational but the Corvette had an international reputation to protect, the very reputation GM had hardly dared to hope for. The rivalry with the Cobra, and the all-too-frequent drubbings it handed out to Corvettes, at racetrack and stoplight alike, were getting to GM's pride. Of course, Shelby's Cobra was an all-out racer, an unruly missile with a monster under the hood. However this monster was not just a Cobra but a Ford.

Ironically, at the time when the Corvette arguably reached its peak, in terms of power, handling, styling and purpose all converging on the definition of a world-class sports car, it had its very bleakest time on the track. Frank Dominianni won B production in 1964, which was all there was for Chevrolet until Allan Barker took it again in 1969. On the other hand, it was during this remarkable period that the Corvette began to sell. From 14,531 units built in 1962, the figure jumped to 21,513 in '63 with the first Sting Ray. 1964 was 22,229, followed by 23,562 in 1965. In 1966 output soared to 27,720, and only fell off a little in 1967 because of a last-minute decision not to change the body shape until 1968. By whatever test you care to apply, the first generation Sting Ray was a car in a class of its own.

CHAPTER 6

1968-1983: MAINSTREAM SPORTSTER

One of the parallel developments that has most influenced the Corvette is GM's tradition of experimental and show cars. And just as the '63 Sting Ray grew from an exotically-styled racer, the 1968 generation began with the Mako Shark II, one of the most impressive and successful styling exercises ever undertaken by the American industry. And, like the racer, the shark was the personal project of William L Mitchell.

Mitchell started work on the Shark immediately after the Sting Ray went into production. By its nature, styling is, in the literal sense, futuristic. Good styling anticipates the future as well as producing it, and that Mitchell's new ideas should seem light years ahead of the car he had just completed should not come as any surprise. Apart from anything else, major styling achievements are always a long time in gestation.

Nonetheless, the Mako Shark II was a great deal more than a surprise: it was a sensation. Mitchell had certain require-

ments of the Mako Shark, and Larry Shinoda's team executed them to perfection: a unity of the upper and lower parts of the car achieved by boldly constructed movement in the mid-section; a finely tapered tail, and an exciting emphasis of the wheels. The elements of its success were certainly visible in the earlier Sting Ray. The Mako Shark drew up the curves over the wheels, underlined the horizontal with gray paintwork that faded gradually into the midnight black of the upper body (the color scheme and some of the styling taken from the Shark, an earlier Mitchell exercise based on what became the '63 Sting Ray), and offset it with the convergence of lines above the rear wheel. Where the Sting Ray had been flat, the Mako Shark was emphatically flat; where the Sting Ray, across its hood, had gracefully inclined, the Mako Shark swooped. In its use of planes, the rear view, from above, was perhaps the most impressive of all, where the sculpted curves were traversed by six beautifully-judged back window louvers. When the Mako Shark II was later restyled as the

Right: The Manta Ray was rather a disappointment following adventurous GM styling exercise, the Mako Shark.

Previous page: The '68 Corvette retained much of the swooping excitement of the experimental Mako Shark II.

Right: The Astro I was far ahead of its time.

Right: Oddly enough the Astro-Vette had a dated look.

Right: Sometimes even GM experiments verge on the downright silly.

Below: The Mako Shark II was a memorable adventure in styling and color.

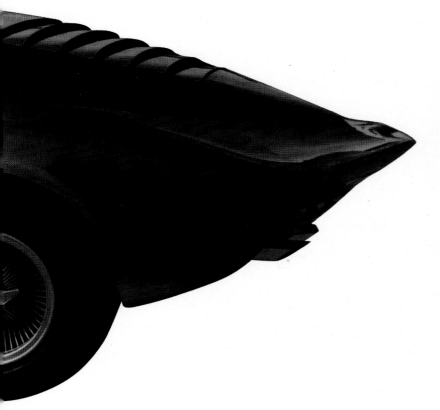

Manta Ray, the back, by comparison, was a mess.

If there is any point in our saga when GM truly lost its nerve with the Corvette, then this is it. The 1968 Corvette was certainly a departure from the earlier models, and certainly it was a lot like the Mako Shark II. But the Mako Shark depended for its success upon a precise execution of line. The '68, a nice, fresh, interesting-looking car to be sure, simply lacked precision. It lacked the tension, for example, between the strong horizontal motif and the voluptuous skyline of the Mako Shark. The curves, in any case, were less daring. The tail was caught between a flip and a chop, and the profile was notched to accept the inset rear window, and thus the exciting confluence of lines above the wheel was lost. Still, it was a good-looking car, and it came with all the customary engines and transmission, from gentleman-shopper to blackout specials, and it also had a detachable sun-roof. In all 28,566 units were built.

In 1969 still more were built: 38,762. The '69 was a slightly better car (and again it was called a Stingray, though it was now a matter of only one word), but of course its sales were based largely on the success of the '68. The Corvette was becoming acceptable in a slightly different way. Perhaps the sports-car market was expanding, or perhaps people no longer saw the Corvette as simply a sports car. Or again, maybe it was just the general spirit of the times.

As it happened, the times were changing. It certainly was not evident in 1969, when Chevrolet offered yet another racing engine, the ZL1, with the Stingray but there would shortly come a time when a sports car would be a renegade in a slightly different and rather less romantic sense. There was also a shift in attitude at GM during the second half of the 1960s. Pete Estes replaced Bunkie Knudsen as general manager of Chevrolet in 1965, and the emphasis was focused more firmly on production. While it was Knudsen who had maneuvered around the AMA and GM's frowning disapproval to get his GS Corvettes on to the race track, it was Estes who put in the third shift at St Louis.

The great personalities were still at GM, and the sports-car inspiration was still in a large measure present (the urge to thrash Ford, for example) but they had all been shuffled around. Even Duntov was no longer in charge of a separate Corvette department. Times were changing, that was all.

A new manager, one John Z DeLorean, took over from Estes in February 1969, and his immediate concern was to see if he could not capitalize on the Corvette's established popularity to hike the price by an average of $500 or so.

The 1970 car was again an improvement in the face of mounting complaints about finish and quality control. There was some squaring-off and tidying-up in the styling, but it was the interior that received most attention. Leather-trimmed seats, door-to-door carpeting and wood-grain trim suddenly gave the Stingray a luxury feel. It was plainly moving away from the purely sporting image of the Sting Ray toward a kind of plushness that was perhaps judged more appropriate for the age. Some shuffling around of the options helped the car's image in terms of value for money. Tinted windows, as well as Positraction differentials, were made standard, and the new Turbo Hydra-Matic automatic transmission was made available as an option at no extra cost.

There was a new engine for 1970, the light, and powerful,

Right: The 1969 model at Le Mans, L88-equipped.

Right: 1969, with L88, in Daytona trim.

Opposite: The '68, in highly dramatic silver.

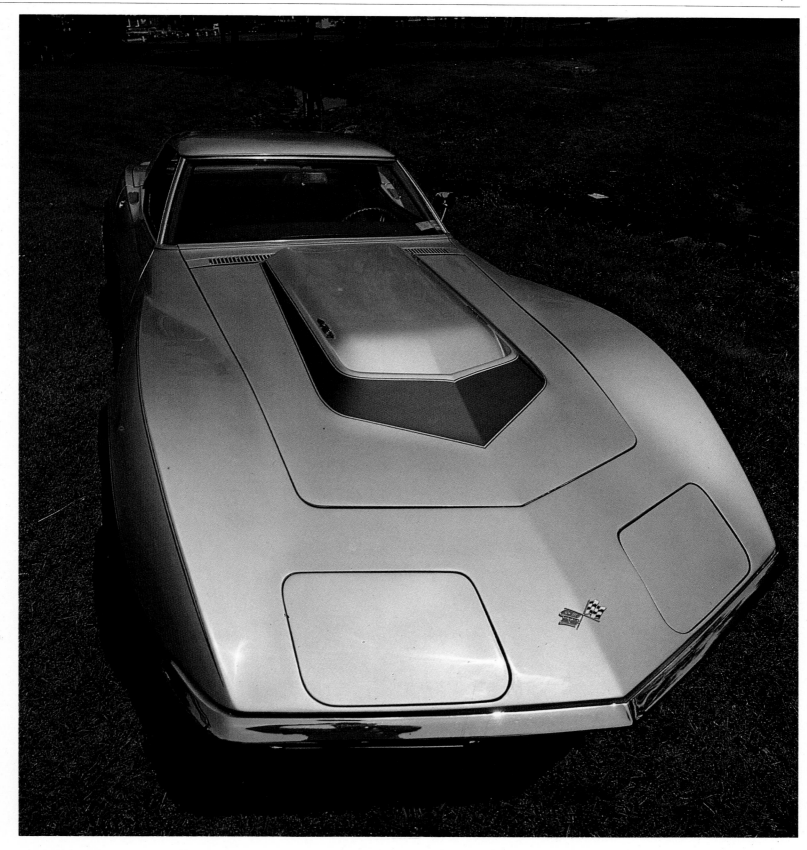

LT-1, but it was introduced against a turning tide. Ed Cole was president of General Motors, and, Corvette lover and racing enthusiast that he was, he insisted that all GM engines should be able to run on fuel of low enough octane rating to be compatible with lead-free gasoline. The catalytic converter was just over the horizon.

The Stingray was substantially unchanged from 1970–73. It was, however, still powerful. Zora Duntov was among those who worked day and night to retain the Corvette's performance in spite of drastically reduced compression ratios. However, Chevrolet was in the grip of a 'de-proliferation' program, cutting out as many expensive and inconvenient options as possible, and by 1972, only three engines were available. Meanwhile, in keeping with the trend to luxury, DeLorean was insisting on much-improved quality control, and getting it.

The 1974 Corvette was equipped with the energy-absorbing impact areas required by Federal regulations. A new suspension option was offered, along with a range of luxurious embellishments such as electric windows, integrated air-conditioning, and stereo-tape decks. 1974 was also the last year of the big-block Mark IV engine. The following year saw the introduction of the catalytic converter, and the consequent detuning of the old faithful 350cid. The

Left and far left: In 1973 the Corvette still looked surprisingly fresh.

Below: The 1970 Corvette, resplendent in Monza Red.

beginning of 1975, perhaps not inappropriately, saw the retirement of Zora Arkus-Duntov, engineer, racer, and, above all, enthusiast. He left a great many enthusiasts behind him, but he left them at work in a very different world.

Sales continued to rise. In 1976, which was simply a year of refinement, Chevrolet built 46,558 Corvettes; by 1977, they were very little short of 50,000. In 1978, which marked 25 years of uninterrupted production of the Corvette, the interior was restyled, and a flush, fastback rear window was added. Chevy also offered, by way of celebration, a brash replica of the official 1978 Indianapolis 500 pace car, which happened to be a Corvette. It was mainly a matter of adding a lumpish spoiler to the rear and giving the '78 a two-tone paint job, but it sold like lightning at prices that soon far exceeded its list figure. The 1979 model, which saw only the most minor adjustments to the standard '78, was perhaps

something of an anticlimax, with no spoilers and no carnival paint job. But by then, production was well above 50,000 units a year.

The spoilers returned in 1980, and were, of course, perfectly ambivalent. Were they there to increase speed, or for aerodynamic fuel-conservation purposes? In a way, it is surprising that spoilers had not appeared earlier in the Corvette's process of adjusting to the new age. The '80 also lost about 250 lbs in the interests of maintaining performance while improving fuel consumption, as America was hit by the oil crisis and became more energy conscious.

The following model year certainly featured some interest-

Below: The 1968–82 model run was as long as it was successful.

Bottom: In 1975 the Corvette was 185.5 inches long, and weighed 3530lbs.

ing developments, though styling and performance were largely unaltered. Weight-saving continued with the introduction of a plastic rear leaf spring. The leaf spring principle survived its own crisis back in 1963, when Duntov's team found that a transverse leaf was more compatible with his design for independent suspension, and that, other than weight, which was not then seen as such a problem, it carried no serious deficiencies as against variable-rate coils. In time it became a monobloc unit, and then it became plastic. Its survival may say something about the tendency to faddishness in engineering trends, however rational and well-considered they may appear at the time. Also interesting in '81 was the fact that only one engine was offered, the L-81 350cid four-barrel carb unit, and the appearance of a computer emission control system. Naturally, the interior was made even more comfortable.

Perhaps the 1982 Corvette was simply a continuation of the '68 line, or perhaps it was the end of the line in more than one sense. In 1982, the Chevrolet Corvette lost the manual gearbox, even as an option. It seemed a break with the past that came close to a slap in the face of the old tradition, the tradition of Louis Chevrolet, of Zora Arkus-Duntov, of Bill Mitchell, and of all the individuals, and all the sporting impulses, that made the Corvette a unique car in the first place. Perhaps it was just common sense, a correct reading of the times allied to a firm grasp of production and sales realities. The day of the sports car was waning and perhaps we need a new word for this sort of car. The '82, after all,

Below: Though somewhat tamed, the 1976 Corvette was still every inch a sports car.

Bottom: Production had risen to 46,588 units by 1976.

Far left: The 25 Years of the Chevrolet Corvette was celebrated by the Anniversary Model, which livened up a long model run.

Left: More celebrations with the Indy Pace Car.

Below: The mature American sports car in 1977.

Far left: The experimental Turbo-Vette of 1980.

Left: The 1980 Corvette, still substantially unchanged, but fully equipped with fashionable spoilers.

Below: The inevitable, the turbocharged Corvette, 1979.

Page 70/71: The 1980 Corvette: maintaining a tradition.

Page 72/73: The Greenwood 1981 Daytona racer and street car.

Below: Still elegant, still fast, but nearing the end of a long production story.

CHEVROLET
USA·1981

Right and below: The 1981 Corvette Daytona still gave room, after all these years, for an exercise in styling flair.

Left: The 1982 Collector Edition.

Below: The 1982 Turbo custom model.

was up 10bhp to 200, and fuel injection was back, an interesting addition to the computer's list of duties.

By way of signing off a model run 14 years long, Chevy offered the 1982 Collector Edition Corvette, mainly a package of trim features and shaded paintwork. It was, however, an attractive package, down to the bronze tinted glass and the leather covered steering wheel, and it came, furthermore, with a frameless hatchback rear window and cast aluminum wheels reminiscent of the first Sting Ray. Like all Corvettes, it was a handsome car.

The '83 is still a front-engined V8. It is lighter, lower, shorter, more economical and, thanks to the power steering, fuel injection, automatic transmission, better instrumentation and better visibility, is easier to drive. It is still a Chevy Corvette, and it is still, supremely, a car of its time. It may be awfully unreasonable to ask for more.

This short review of the history of the Chevy Corvette, of

the men, of the ideas, of the inspirations, of the times that made it what it was, ends with the fifth generation. We will continue to refer to the Corvette as America's only true sports car, almost regardless of what becomes of it. In 1957, the Corvette was certainly a sports car. In 1963 it was a sports car with race-winning potential. But as times changed, our ways of looking at cars changed with them and so has the Chevy Corvette.

One last word on the question of sports cars. While the Corvette was developing its fifth generation, Corvette owners went racing. Chevy Corvettes won SCCA A production in 1969, 1970, 1971, 1972, 1974, 1975, 1976, 1977, and 1978. They won B production in 1969, 1970, 1971, 1972, 1973, 1974, 1976, 1977, 1978, 1979, and 1980. This is in part how the Corvette meets the definition of sports car, and it may be something the Corvettes of the future will find a trifle hard to follow.

CHAPTER 7

1984: A GENERATION ON: STILL FAST— STILL BEAUTIFUL

While the production lines were being readied for the fifth Corvette. General Motors was preparing to establish itself as the styling leader of the 1980s. Almost inevitably, much of this effort centered on the Corvette, and the team led by Zora Duntov. In many ways, GM was simply responding to the natural role of the sports car in the auto industry. It is, afer all, the sports car, and not the family saloon, that does the industry's high-altitude, experimental work. Its definition somehow includes the notion of the free spirit. In this respect, GM has always put its sports car to particularly good use.

Duntov's team was taken by the idea of a mid-engined car, and, working with some of the lessons learned in his experimental racer, CERV II, began work on a project known as XP-882. It was impressive, but it would have been dangerously costly to produce. Not unreasonably, John DeLorean canceled it.

There the matter might have rested, with the XP-882 in mothballs, except for the news that Ford was about to throw a

Previous page: The 1983 Corvette was a beautifully styled car, which built on and extended the fine tradition of the GM sports car.

Below: The 1984 Corvette emphasizes practicality as well as style. Glamorous, but accessible.

Left: The rear profile of 1984 model shows the unity of style that has become the Corvette hallmark.

Bill Mitchell's four-rotor: one of the finest-looking sports cars ever. It first appeared at the Paris Show in 1973.

Far right: Gull-wing doors and a pair of rotary engines made the four-rotor a trifle impractical.

Above: The 1984 Corvette is 176.5 inches long, with a wheelbase of 96.2 inches.

Right: Thirty years is a long time but a Corvette is a Corvette.

mid-engined sensation into the arena of the New York Show. Furthermore, the American Motor Corporation were said to have something similar in mind. The XP-882 was dusted down and practically rushed to New York, where it was displayed without comment as a prototype Corvette. Since then, the world has waited, in vain, for a mid-engine Corvette. No matter. What was important by that time was less what GM could and would produce, than what it was possible to produce, to imagine, to conjure up, with the blend of engineering and styling talents at GM's disposal.

Next came the two-rotor, a car using a Wankel rotary engine, and then, almost immediately, the four-rotor, using two Wankels, coupled by Duntov. The two-rotor, oddly enough, was built on a Porsche 914 chassis and partially styled, in Italy, by Carrozeria Pininfarina. It was, of course, a good-looking car. It is said that John DeLorean was anxious to have Giorgetto Giugiaro style the four-rotor, and that Bill Mitchell hit back — with everything he had. His department, he told GM, would style the new car, and it would style it in such a way that the automobile industry would never forget it. The two cars appeared for the first time at the Paris Show in 1973. The two-rotor was remarkable for the percipience and execution of its style; the four-rotor was perhaps the most beautiful car the world had ever seen.

GM tired of the whole idea of rotary engines, and the four-rotor was shelved. About a year later, it was rolled out and equipped with a 400cid V8. It was renamed, perfectly, the

Aerovette. The Aerovette is, and perhaps will always be, the final word on the Chevrolet Corvette. Because it is everything a sports car could possibly be, and because it bears the most eloquent possible witness to the tradition of which it is so supremely a part. The Aerovette appeared at much the same time as Zora Arkus-Duntov retired. It bore his mark. It bore the mark, too, of Bill Mitchell, Ed Cole, Clare MacKichan, Bob McLean, Larry Shinoda, Harley Earl; and in its shadow stand the racers as well as the engineers, John Fitch, Dick Thompson, Piero Taruffi, and Louis Chevrolet.

Whatever becomes of the production Corvette, whatever shapes it takes in response to market surveys and production necessities, whatever power it produces in response to what people need and the way things are, it will continue to be subject not only to a spirit, but a standard: the standard of aesthetic and engineering excellence which has guided its development, in spite of everything, for 30 years. Not every Corvette has been a perfect car, or even a good car. But they have all been special cars because the people who made them always had something to say about the way a car ought to be.

Even so, one cannot help but feel there might be another explanation of why, for more than 30 years, General Motors, mainstream Detroit, produced a car that was, by any accepted industry standards, wildly eccentric, an enthusiasts' fantasy in V8 and fiberglass. Could it be that the Corvette endured because it flew in the face of every dictum that ever made a penny for Henry Ford?

CHAPTER 8

BEYOND THE CORVETTE: A PORTFOLIO

Previous page: Few cars have lent themselves as easily to inspired customising as the Corvette.

Far left: Borrowing the louver theme from some of GM's own experiments, this car also makes forceful use of color.

Left: Inevitably, engines have been heavily modified.

Far left: Still, unmistakably, a Corvette.

Left: Light shade emphasizes the engine hump, while clever bodywork tucks away the headlamps without impairing the sleek lines of the nose.

Classical geometric precision paintwork – a fitting reflection of the engineering philosophy behind a generation of Chevrolet Corvettes.

ACKNOWLEDGMENTS
The Publishers would like to thank Mr
Martyn L Schorr of Performance Media
and the Chevrolet Motor Division for
the use of many of the pictures in this
book, which have come from his
private collection.